This Boxer Books paperback belongs to

. . . .

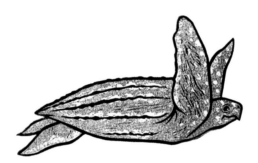

www.boxerbooks.com

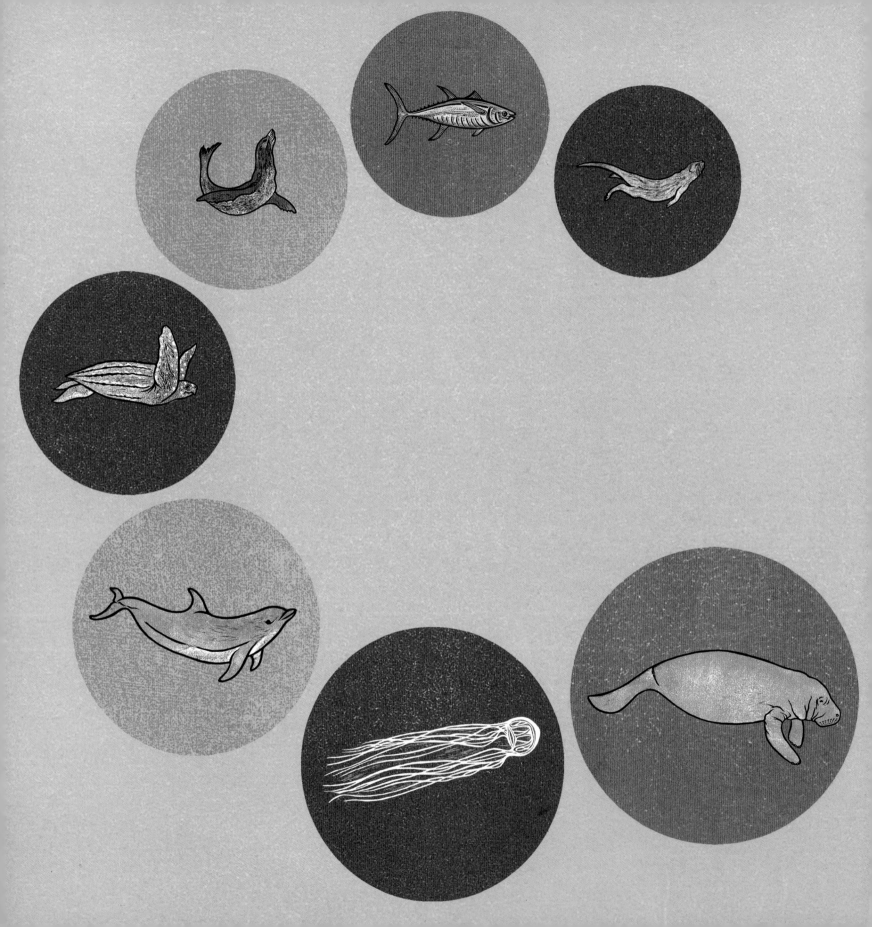

For Thomas, Henry and Miriam, I hope you enjoy exploring nature as much as I always have. A.L. x

First published in Great Britain in 2017 by Boxer Books Limited.
First published in paperback in 2018 by Boxer Books Limited.
www.boxerbooks.com

Boxer® is a registered trademark of Boxer Books Limited.

Text and illustrations copyright © 2017 Alison Limentani
The right of Alison Limentani to be identified as the author and illustrator of this work has
been asserted by her in accordance with the Copyright, Designs and Patents Act, 1988.
All rights reserved, including the right of reproduction in whole or in part in any form.
A catalogue record for this book is available from the British Library.

The illustrations were all relief printed using collographs and lino cuts.
The text is set in Futura.

ISBN 978-1-910716-51-9

1 3 5 7 9 10 8 6 4 2

Printed in China

All of our papers are sourced from managed forests and renewable resources.

How Long
is a Whale?

Alison Limentani

Boxer Books

10 sea otters

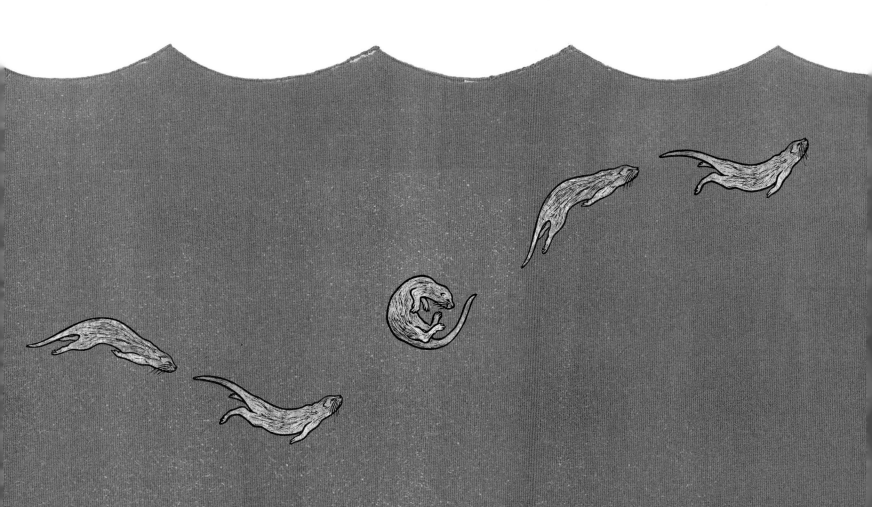

are as long as

9 yellowfin tuna,

which are as long as

8 California sea lions,

which are as long as

7 leatherback
sea turtles,

which are as long as

6 bottlenose dolphins,

which are as long as

5 box jellyfish,

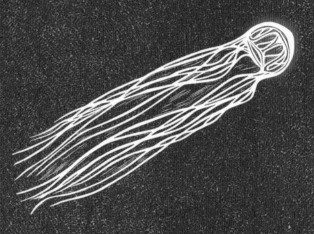

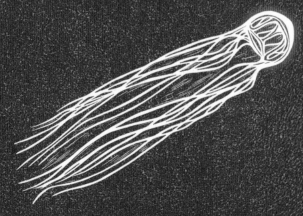

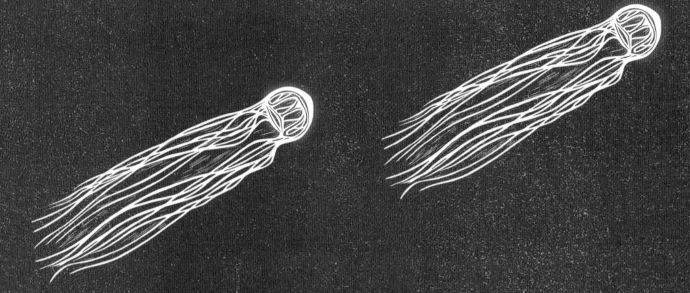
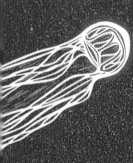

which are as long as

4 West Indian manatees,

which are as long as

3 great white sharks,

which are as long as

2 killer whales,

which are as long as

1 humpback whale

but . . .

2 humpback whales

are as long as

and 3 leatherback sea turtles

1 great white shark
and 2 bottlenose dolphins

1 blue whale,

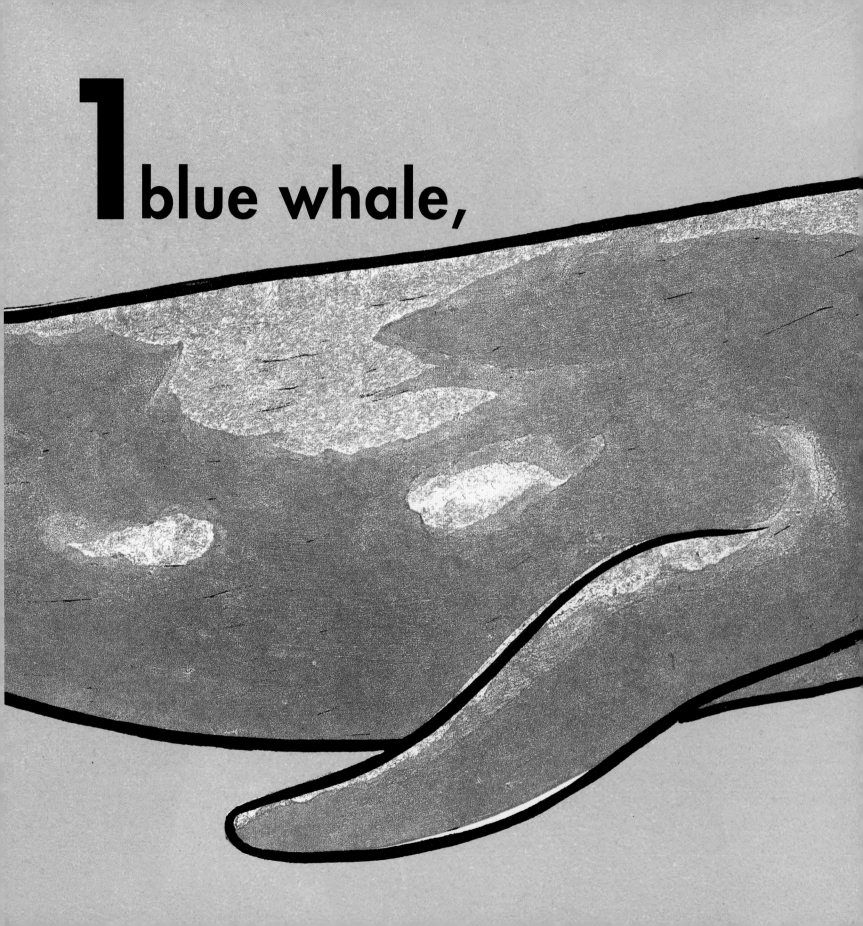

which is as long as . . .

and 5 sea otters.

and 4 yellowfin tuna

1.9m

California
sea lion

1.7m

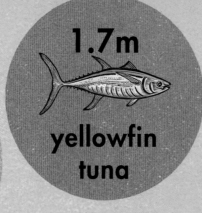

yellowfin
tuna

1.5m

sea otter

2.1m

leatherback
sea turtle

Different animals of the same species can vary in length, just as different people vary in height. All the lengths in this book are based on animals within the healthy adult range.

2.5m

bottlenose
dolphin

3.0m

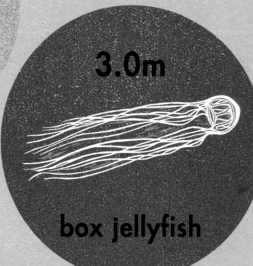

box jellyfish

3.8m

West Indian
manatee

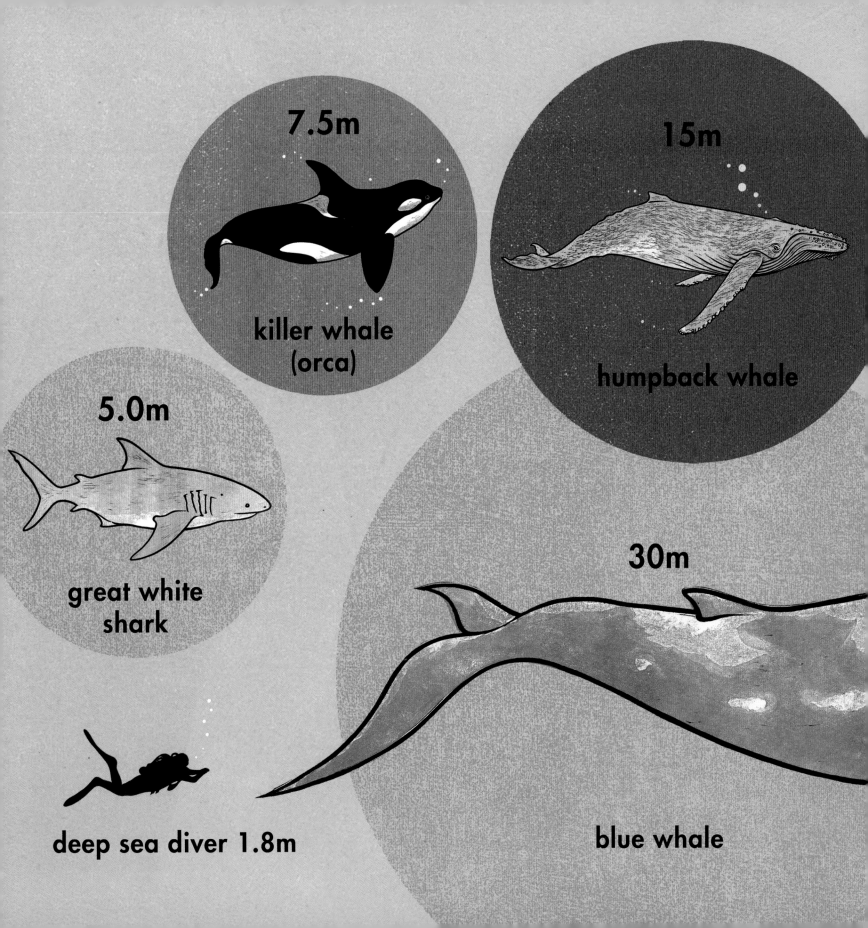

7.5m

killer whale
(orca)

15m

humpback whale

5.0m

great white
shark

30m

deep sea diver 1.8m

blue whale

More Boxer Books to enjoy

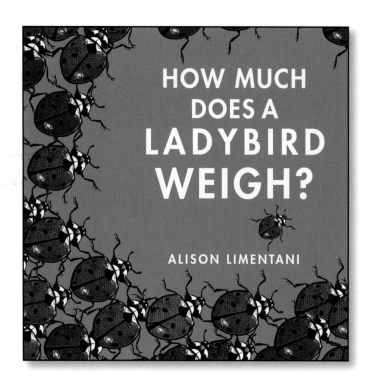

HOW MUCH DOES A LADYBIRD WEIGH?
by Alison Limentani

Have you ever wondered how much a ladybird weighs? What about the weight of a snail, a bird or even a swan? In Alison Limentani's extraordinary and original picture book she introduces us to a fascinating world of numbers, weight and wildlife.

HOW TALL WAS A T.REX?
by Alison Limentani

Have you ever wondered what a T.rex was really like? How tall was it? How much did it eat? Did it have scales or feathers? Find out lots of fascinating facts in this brilliant exploration of the world's scariest dinosaur, the T.rex!

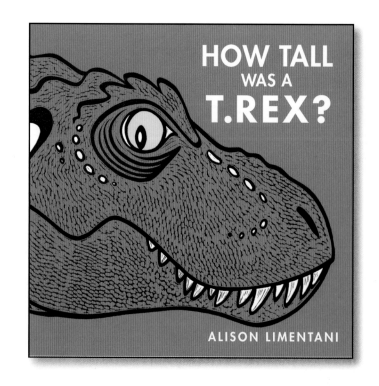